Introduction

***If you were going to paint a picture of yourself,
how would you do it?***

Would you look in the mirror? Or would you paint yourself from memory? Would you get all dressed up? Would you wear your pajamas? Or would you dress up like somebody else? Would you paint yourself smiling, or looking very serious? Would you paint your entire body, or just your head?

These are just some of the questions the artists in this book considered before they made pictures of themselves—pictures that are called self-portraits.

Looking at self-portraits is a great way to learn about different artists. For example, you can see what style they were using at the time, what kind of clothes they wore, and even what they thought about themselves.

But if there's one thing you'll find out from reading this book, it's this: Every artist has his or her own way of making a self-portrait. And that's what makes looking at them so much fun.

Self-Portrait of 1484 at the Age of Thirteen
Graphische Sammlung Albertina, Vienna

Albrecht Dürer
(1471-1528)

In 1484, in the town of Nuremberg, Germany,
a thirteen-year-old boy drew this picture of himself.
It is the first known self-portrait in the history of art.
The boy's name was Albrecht Dürer.

Albrecht grew up to be one of the greatest artists of his time. There is a story that one of his self-portraits was so lifelike, his dog barked and wagged its tail upon seeing it for the first time.

Even though Albrecht lived more than 500 years ago, more than 1,000 pieces of his work, including oil paintings, water-colors, woodcuts, engravings, and drawings, have survived to this day. Albrecht seemed to know that later generations would be interested in his art, so he saved what he could. He inscribed much of it with his distinctive monogram, a small letter "D" under the crossbar of a larger letter "A." Sometimes he even wrote short notes on his work to help explain it.

For example, years after he drew this self-portrait, Albrecht added these words in the upper-right-hand corner: "This I drew, using a mirror; it is my own likeness, in the year 1484, when I was still a child." It sounds as if he was proud of what he had done, and we can see why.

Bernardino Campi Painting
Sofonisba Anguissola (c. 1560)
Pinacoteca Nazionale, Siena

Sofonisba Anguissola
(1532–1625)

OK, here's a trick question: Can a self-portrait be a self-portrait if someone other than the artist paints it? In this case, the answer is yes.

Sofonisba Anguissola lived in Italy during the 1500s. When she was fourteen years old, her father sent her to study painting with an artist named Bernardino Campi, who taught Sofonisba for three years. Some years later, Sofonisba painted this picture of Bernardino painting her. Why do you think she showed herself being painted by someone else?

Very simply, this painting is Sofonisba's tribute to her teacher. She wanted to thank Bernardino for everything he had taught her. By showing herself being painted by him, Sofonisba was giving him credit for making her into an artist. And by leaving her portrait unfinished in the painting, she was letting him know that she was still unfinished as an artist, and that she would continue to learn and improve.

Artemisia Gentileschi
(1593–1652)

What does this self-portrait of Artemisia Gentileschi have in common with the Statue of Liberty? If you said that both are women, you're on the right track. The answer is, both are allegories.

An allegory is a symbol, often a person, that stands for something else. For example, the Statue of Liberty is the woman who stands for freedom. In this self-portrait, Artemisia Gentileschi painted herself as Pittura, the woman who stands for the art of painting.

According to mythology, Pittura invented painting. And around her neck, on a gold chain, she wore the "mask of imitation"—just as Artemisia is wearing it in this painting. So why did she paint herself as Pittura?

Artemisia lived in Italy at a time when women were discouraged from becoming painters. They were expected to stay at home and raise families. But Artemisia's father was a painter, and he taught her everything he knew. In fact, Artemisia learned to paint before she learned to read. By painting herself as Pittura, Artemisia was telling the people who didn't think she should be a painter, "No one can keep me from painting. Painting is what I do. Painting is who I am."

Self-Portrait as La Pittura (c. 1630)
The Royal Collection, Hampton Court Palace

Las Meninas (1656)
Museo del Prado, Madrid

Diego Velázquez
(1599-1660)

Yes, you are looking at a self-portrait, although at first glance you might not even notice that the artist, Diego Velázquez, is in the painting at all.

That's because the focus of his painting is on the little blonde-haired girl, Princess Margarita of Spain. She looks as if she has just arrived in the room with her playmates and her maids of honor. In the shadows to the left of her is Diego, who stands in front of a huge canvas with his palette and brushes. But why does everyone in the painting seem to be looking at us?

The answer is in the mirror on the wall behind Diego, where we can see the reflections of the King and Queen. For them to be seen in this mirror, they must be standing right where we stand when we look at this painting. This means that the people in the painting aren't looking at us, they're looking at the King and Queen (Margarita's father and mother) posing for Diego.

With this painting, Diego is showing us how proud he is to be the court painter of Spain's royal family. But by hiding himself off to the side, he is also letting us know that they will always be more important than he is.

Jan Vermeer
(1632-1675)

This painting might be a self-portrait of the Dutch artist Jan Vermeer. Then again, it might not. After all, we can't even see the artist's face.

The painting itself is like a play. In the front hangs a curtain, which has been pulled aside to reveal the stage—an artist's studio. On this stage are two actors, a man playing the part of the artist and a woman playing the part of his model. The model is dressed up as Clio, who symbolizes history. And next to the curtain is a chair, an invitation for the audience (us) to sit down and watch the artist paint Clio—in other words, to watch history being made.

The question is, do you think the artist is Jan? If it is, then he was playing a joke on us, because we can see only his back. And because none of Jan's other surviving paintings are self-portraits, we will probably never know what he looked like.

Maybe Jan was modest, and he never did a self-portrait. Or maybe he did one and it was lost. But for anyone who wants to know what he looked like, this painting is all the more intriguing.

The Art of Painting (The Artist's Studio) (1665–1666)
Kunsthistorisches Museum, Vienna

Francisco de Goya
(1746-1828)

In 1786, the Spanish painter Francisco de Goya was named Painter to the King. This was good news, for it meant Francisco would receive a steady income.

But it also meant he was busier than he had ever been.

Francisco was a fast painter. He liked to work directly on the canvas without doing preliminary studies. He made short, rapid brushstrokes and did very little retouching. He often painted for ten hours at a time. But at one point he said in a letter, "I am so up to my ears at this moment that I do not know which way to turn and especially how to fulfill all the engagements I have accepted."

This self-portrait shows us one way that Francisco kept up. We see him standing in front of his easel, elegantly dressed, staring intently at his model. And on his head he wears a hat with candles stuck in the brim.

So, long before the invention of electric light, Francisco de Goya figured out how to paint at night. And from this self-portrait, it looks as if he is happy to let us in on his secret.

Self-Portrait Painting in His Studio (c.1790–1795)
Museo de la Real Academia de Bellas Artes de San Fernando, Madrid

Myself. Portrait-Landscape (1890)
National Gallery, Prague

Henri Rousseau
(1844-1910)

Henri Rousseau considered himself the greatest painter of his time, even though he never had any training as an artist and didn't become a full-time painter until he was forty years old,

His self-confidence was particularly notable given the fact that artists like Pablo Picasso, Paul Cezanne, and Wassily Kandinsky were his contemporaries! Henri taught himself how to paint by copying works in the Louvre and by studying nature at the botanical gardens in Paris. And even though other artists often made fun of him, they also admired his hard work and determination.

In this self-portrait, Henri painted himself in the center of the canvas, very large and dressed in black. This makes everything in the Paris landscape behind him seem small and unimportant. He stands taller than the ship, taller than the Eiffel Tower peeking out from behind the ship— even taller than the hot-air balloon!

But there is more to this self-portrait. Written upside down on his palette are two names: Clemence, his first wife, who had died two years earlier, and Josephine, who later became his second wife. With this small gesture, Henri seems to be letting us know, and reminding himself, that without the support of these two women, he wouldn't be a painter at all.

Self-Portrait with Bandaged Ear (1889)
Courtauld Institute Galleries, London

Vincent van Gogh
(1853-1890)

Vincent van Gogh was a painter for just ten years of his short life. But during those ten years he made more than 800 paintings—and more than thirty self-portraits!

Because he sold only one painting during his lifetime, Vincent couldn't afford to hire models. In one of many letters to his brother, Theo, Vincent wrote, "I purposely bought a mirror good enough to enable me to work from my image . . . because if I can manage to paint the colouring of my own head . . . I shall likewise be able to paint the heads of other good souls, men and women."

Unfortunately, Vincent suffered from mental illness late in his life, and this made it harder and harder for him to paint. It even caused him to cut off his own ear. One month after that incident, he made this portrait of himself wearing a bandage around his head. It's January, so he also wears a hat and coat. Behind him is his easel, and on the wall, is one of his favorite Japanese prints.

The year after he made this self-portrait, Vincent died. As he wrote in another letter to Theo, "They say . . . it is difficult to know yourself—but it isn't easy to paint yourself either." Difficult as it was, Vincent succeeded.

Self-Portrait with Seven Fingers (1912–1913)
Stedelijk Museum of Modern Art, Amsterdam

Marc Chagall
(1887–1985)

The first time you look at this self-portrait,
you might think Marc Chagall had seven fingers
on his left hand. Either that, or he couldn't count.
But what's the real story?

Marc grew up in a Jewish village in Russia. As a young man, he left Russia to study art in Paris. But he took with him fond memories of his childhood. And he never forgot where he came from.

In this self-portrait, Marc painted himself at work in his Paris studio. You can see the Eiffel Tower through the window behind him. And above his easel, you can see Marc's memories of his village, floating in a cloud. He is referring to these memories as he makes the painting in front of him.

So why does he have seven fingers? According to an old Jewish expression, doing something with seven fingers means doing it very fast and very well. With this self-portrait, Marc seems to be saying that even though he still thinks about his home in Russia, he is glad he moved to Paris because moving here has made him a better painter— in other words, a painter with seven fingers.

Norman Rockwell
(1894-1978)

***How many self-portraits can you find
in this painting? If you said three, you have
a lot more looking to do.***

Norman Rockwell called this painting Triple Self-Portrait, but if you look at the easel above his head, you can see a piece of paper with four more self-portraits in sketch form. That makes seven. And stuck to the other side of the easel are the self-portraits of four other artists: Albrecht Dürer, Rembrandt van Rijn, Pablo Picasso, and Vincent van Gogh. These were Norman's heroes, the artists who inspired him. Their self-portraits, added to Norman's seven, make eleven self-portraits in all.

You'll also notice that Norman's face looks different in the painting than it does in the mirror. For example, in the painting he's not wearing glasses and looks a little younger. Perhaps this was Norman's way of showing us that sometimes artists paint things the way they want them to be, rather than the way they really are. And that includes pictures of themselves.

Triple Self-Portrait (1960)
The Norman Rockwell Museum at Stockbridge, Massachusetts

Hand with Reflecting Sphere (1935)
Cordon Art-Baarn, Netherlands

M. C. Escher
(1898-1972)

During his lifetime, Maurits Cornelis Escher made more than 400 lithographs, woodcuts, and wood engravings and more than 2,000 drawings and sketches. But his most popular picture of all may be this unusual self-portrait.

Maurits drew himself sitting in his studio in Rome, holding a reflecting sphere in his hand. This sphere reflects not only the image of Maurits but also the entire inside of his studio. It's the kind of playful, mind-bending picture that he is famous for.

Now for a question that looks easy, but isn't: With which hand is Maurits holding the reflecting sphere? Before you answer, here is a clue: This self-portrait is a lithographic print, and a lithographic print is a mirror image of what the artist actually draws.

If you said that he's holding the sphere with his right hand, you're correct! Maurits was left-handed (like Leonardo da Vinci and Michelangelo Buonarroti), so in order to draw the sphere with his left hand, he would have to hold it in his right.

Jacob Lawrence
(1917–2000)

Jacob Lawrence grew up in the black community of Harlem, in New York City. He first became interested in art as a twelve-year-old boy at a local arts and crafts program.

He later trained at the Harlem Art Workshop. Not surprisingly, Jacob's earliest paintings show life on the streets of Harlem. As Jacob matured as an artist, he began painting stories from black history. For example, he did a series of paintings about Frederick Douglass, the orator and writer. Another series featured Harriet Tubman and the Underground Railroad. Then in 1971, Jacob was offered a position as a professor of art at the University of Washington, and he moved to Seattle.

But Jacob always remembered his Harlem roots. In this self-portrait, we see him in his Seattle studio, surrounded by his paintings. Jacob stands at the top of the stairs leading up to the studio, which symbolizes his climb from his beginnings as a poor boy to his present as a respected painter and teacher.

And behind him, through the window of his Seattle studio, we see a city. But it is not Seattle. It is Harlem.

The Studio (1977)
Seattle Art Museum

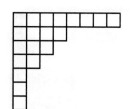
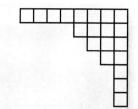

Chuck Close
(1940–)

From a distance, this self-portrait of Chuck Close looks like a photograph. But if you get close enough, it magically transforms into a bunch of colorful squares with funny shapes inside.

Chuck has always been interested in faces. He prefers to paint the faces of people he knows, like his family, his artist friends, or himself. And he likes to work big.

Chuck starts by taking a photo of the person he wants to paint. Then he divides the photo into a grid of squares and repaints the photo onto his canvas, one square at a time. Each square becomes its own tiny work of art. As Chuck himself describes it, "I build a painting by putting little marks together—some look like hot dogs, some like doughnuts."

Since 1988, when he became paralyzed after a serious illness, Chuck has worked from a wheelchair, with a brush strapped to his arm. His portraits have become looser and more colorful as a result. But there is one thing you can say about all his work—it grabs your attention. As Chuck says, "You're looking at it, it's looking at you."

Self-Portrait, 2000
Pace Prints, New York

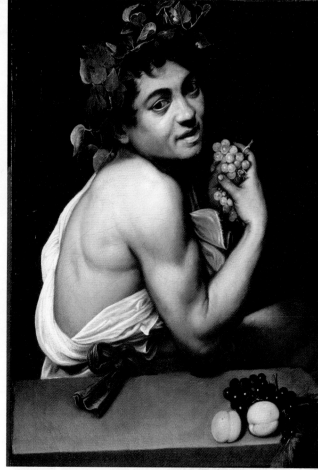

Untitled, #224 (1990)
Metro Pictures, New York

Sick Bacchus (c. 1593–1594)
Galleria Borghese, Rome

Cindy Sherman
(1954–)

Cindy Sherman is a photographer. She takes pictures of herself. Yet she doesn't consider these pictures to be self-portraits. Why not?

A self-portrait should reveal something about you. But Cindy's pictures don't reveal much about her at all. Using makeup and costumes, she dresses up like different kinds of people, then photographs herself. As Cindy describes it, "I am trying to make people recognize something of themselves rather than me."

This photo is a good example. As you can see, Cindy is dressed up like Bacchus, the Greek god of wine, from Caravaggio's famous painting. The funny thing is, Caravaggio's painting is a self-portrait. He painted himself dressed up like Bacchus. So Cindy's picture is actually the photo of a woman (herself) who is dressed up like the painting of a man (Caravaggio) who is dressed up like a Greek god (Bacchus). Talk about a mind-bender!

With this picture, Cindy seems to be asking us several questions: What does it mean to "pose" for your picture? How much of your real self can be captured in a painting, or even in a photograph? And what exactly is a self-portrait anyway? Your answers to these questions, like a good self-portrait, will reveal something about you.

Photo Credits